FROM BR TO BEECHING
VOLUME TWO

Four Coupled
PART ONE

by **PATRICK WHITEHOUSE** and D

GW00368105

FRONT COVER
Class E4 2-4-0 No. 62785 waits at Mildenhall with a train for Cambridge in May 1958.
J. G. Dewing/Colour Rail.

REAR COVER TOP
SE&C Class D 4-4-0 No. 31075 near North Camp with a Reading-Redhill service in October 1956.
T. B. Owen/Colour Rail.

REAR COVER BOTTOM
NBR Class D34 4-4-0 No. 62478 *Glen Quoich* passes Haymarket shed at the head of a local train for Crail in 1957. J. Robertson/Colour Rail.

ISBN 0-906899-41-9

FIRST PUBLISHED 1990

© TEXT:
Patrick Whitehouse, David Jenkinson and Millbrook House Ltd.

PHOTOGRAPHS:
As credited.

DESIGNED BY
BARNABUS DESIGN & PRINT · TRURO · CORNWALL

TYPESET BY
TYPESTYLE · TRURO · CORNWALL

PRINTED BY
CENTURY LITHO · PENRYN · CORNWALL

BOUND BY
BOOTHS BOOKBINDERS · PENRYN · CORNWALL

PUBLISHED BY
ATLANTIC TRANSPORT PUBLISHERS
TREVITHICK HOUSE · WEST END
PENRYN · CORNWALL TR10 8HE

CONTENTS

AUTHORS' INTRODUCTION

In presenting this, the second of our 'BR to Beeching' series, we are conscious that the steam locomotive with four coupled wheels has the most honourable of all pedigrees. After all, the very first successful steam locomotive (that built by Richard Trevithick to launch the steam locomotive era at Pen-y-darren in 1804) was of this kind. From then until almost the end of steam, there was always a place for engines with no more than four driven wheels. In fact, the history of the four-coupled engine could, in a very real sense, also be seen to mirror the whole history of the steam locomotive itself.

For this reason, we are delighted that John Powell, that well known latter-day steam locomotive engineer and author, has agreed to write an appraisal of the 4-4-0 by way of introduction to our survey of these types. We are indeed indebted to him for supporting our endeavours. Our thanks too go, once again, to John Edgington and John Smart both for their indefatigable picture research and for their valued contribution to the caption writing.

By the time of our survey, the most common arrangement to be seen in Britain was the familiar 4-4-0 type, most of which had been built for passenger use. As a result, they mostly displayed large driving wheels. But there were some smaller-wheeled 4-4-0 survivors of a quasi-mixed traffic kind, not to mention the few examples of both the older 2-4-0 and 0-4-2 arrangements and the later 4-4-2 type. Most of these appear in our survey and, in fact, so many different types of four-coupled engines were still to be seen on all manner of duties during 1948-63 that we have felt obliged to split our review into two parts of which this is the first.

The engines and workings featured both in this and the companion volume embrace just about every conceivable approach to the problem. Some were very modern, by steam standards; others went back into the 19th Century, such was the popularity and longevity of the idea. There were many early approaches but by the time of the final steam era, the only surviving arrangement was to connect the driven axle to the adjacent one by means of side (coupling) rods attached to the outer face of the of wheels. It is this type with which we are solely concerned here.

Examples of most later strands of development could still be seen in the final years of British steam, offering a fascinating 'live' history lesson for those who had eyes to see. Since a main object of this survey is to reveal how much of it survived to the very end, we are fortunate indeed that so many photographers chose to point their cameras at these, often by now, lesser-lights. There were also very many 'sub-plots' within the main story, so for ease of understanding we have chosen to amplify this general outline in the form of a brief introductory essay to each of the categories featured. For much the same reason, we have also chosen to gather the few remaining 2-4-0s and 0-4-2s together in this first part, while the 4-4-2s will likewise all appear together in the sequel.

Finally, we should point out that to be truly representative, we have at times felt obliged to use less than perfect pictures to illustrate the story. We have therefore, and quite deliberately in some cases, resisted the temptation to put pure pictorial appeal above historical significance; we trust that our readers will understand why.

Patrick Whitehouse   **David Jenkinson**

The Surviving 2-4-0s and 0-4-2s

Only four basic designs lasted into Nationalisation, one Midland 2-4-0 (the three survivors all had different wheel diameters and were nominally from different classes), one Great Western 2-4-0 (absorbed from the Midland & South Western Junction Railway), one Great Eastern 2-4-0 design and one London & South Western 0-4-2. They were very much Victorian engines (the LSWR 0-4-2s were known as the Jubilees after Queen Victoria's Golden Jubilee) once beautifully liveried and polished but now eking out their lives as station pilots or over branch lines needing low axle loadings. The Midland engines were by far the oldest, the MSWJ the youngest and the Great Eastern E4s the most useful; one has been preserved in the National Collection. They were all anachronisms before World War II but this gave them perhaps ten years extra life – maybe more for the E4s whose branch line work lasted a little longer until the coming of the DMU or closure.

The surviving examples are summarised at Table 1 below.

Midland Railway 6ft 9in 2-4-0 No. 20216 Johnson Class 1P acting as station pilot at Cheltenham Lansdown in August 1949. This was one of only three MR 2-4-0s to come into BR stock. No. 20216 was built at Derby in 1879 and was numbered 1409 as a member of the 1400 Class. In the general Midland renumbering of 1907 it became 216 which number it carried until 1934 when to avoid confusion with LMS standard classes it became 20216. No. 216 was rebuilt with a G6 Belpaire boiler c.1926. Withdrawal was in November 1949. The shed plate reads 22B, Gloucester Barnwood. BR number 58022 was allocated but never carried. (P. B. Whitehouse/Millbrook House Collection)

Type Origin and Class	TABLE 1: 2-4-0 and 0-4-2 locomotives taken into BR stock on 1st January 1948.														
	1948	1949	1950	1951	1952	1953	1954	1955	1956	1957	1958	1959	1960	1961	1962
2-4-0															
MR 1P (6'3", 6'6", 6'9")	3	2	1												
GER E4	18	18	18	18	18	18	18	16	10	5	3	1			
MSWJR	3	3	3	3	3	1	1								
0-4-2															
LSWR A12 'Jubilee'	4														

Above: The Great Eastern Intermediate 2-4-0, later LNER class E4 and first built in 1891, proved to be a long lived and useful design. Eighteen of this 5ft 8in mixed traffic type survived into BR days and none were withdrawn before November 1954, a reflection both of the low priority given to upgrading the motive power in East Anglia and the fact that they were ideally suited to the long cross-country routes, having a relatively light maximum axle load of 14 tons 3 cwt, unusually carried by the leading wheels. No. 62786 (1/95-7/56) is seen here at Cavendish, Suffolk with a Marks Tey-Cambridge train via Long Melford and Haverhill on 21st May 1951. Note dual Westinghouse/vacuum brake fittings. The locomotive is allocated to Cambridge shed (31A). The coaches are ex-GER types with a corridor brake leading. (P. M. Alexander/Millbrook House Collection)

Right: E4 No. 62781 (11/92-1/56) leaves Marks Tey with a midday Cambridge-Colchester train on 18th June 1949; it is coming out of the branch platform onto the main line. Note the side window cab which it received in August 1936 when allocated to Barnard Castle for working over the Stainmore route to Tebay and Penrith. The loco headed back to its home depot with the 4.30 pm to Cambridge. (P. M. Alexander/Millbrook House Collection)

Three Midland & South Western Junction Railway locomotives survived into BR ownership, all were Dubs 2-4-0s built in 1894, MSWJ Nos. 10-12, GWR/BR Nos. 1334-6. The locomotives were all rebuilt with GW standard No. 11 boilers in 1924 and transferred away from their home ground to work on the Lambourn Valley line where they were often employed on horse box specials. The class finally became extinct in March 1954 when No. 1336 was withdrawn.

Above: In the first view, No. 1334 (1894-9/52) stands in the stock shed at Swindon around the time of its withdrawal. Its allocation was Didcot (DID/81E) and it was normally sub-shedded at Newbury, the other two members of the class being at Reading (81D).

Below: In their last years the MSWJ 2-4-0s were in demand for special trains and in the second view, No. 1335 (1894-9/52) waits to take an SLS special from Oxford out of Moreton-in-Marsh station up the Shipston-on-Stour branch on Sunday 31st August 1952 a matter of days before withdrawal. The branch had closed to passengers in July 1929 but lingered on until final extinction in May 1960. No. 1335 was the only one of its type to receive a BR smokebox door numberplate. The shedplate reads 81D (Reading). (P. M. Alexander/Millbrook House Collection)

Above: The Adams Class A12 6ft 1in 0-4-2 design, first built in 1887 and collectively known as 'The Jubilees' in commemoration of Queen Victoria's Golden Jubilee, was one of the earlier examples of the mixed traffic locomotive. Their versatility and simplicity had justified retention through the Second World War; however the end of hostilities saw most of those remaining (29 at 31st December 1945) laid aside. Four were taken into BR stock Nos, 618, 627, 629 and 636. All were withdrawn within a year.

This photograph, taken just outside the period, shows A12 No. 643 (3/93-7/47) at Guildford shed on 11th April 1947. It carries a Drummond boiler. Also visible on shed are two Class M7 0-4-4 tanks Nos. 60 and 676. (P. M. Alexander/Millbrook House Collection)

Left: The final survivor. Class A12 No. 629 (built 1/1893) was withdrawn from Eastleigh in December 1948 and is seen here on Eastleigh dump in January 1949. (P. M. Alexander/Millbrook House Collection)

Introduction to and Summary of the 4-4-0 Types

by A. J. Powell

The 4-4-0 had a very long innings in Britain, even though the arrangement originated in the USA and was actually *patented* there in 1836. In the nineteenth century it became so ubiquitous there, in outside cylinder form, that the type was given the generic name "American", as well known as the "Pacific" or "Mikado".

Here it started with tank engines by Gooch for the GWR in 1849, and as a tender engine on the Stockton & Darlington in 1860. It was rapidly developed, usually as an inside cylinder machine until by the first decade of the new century it was *the* choice for express passenger work. Its virtue was that it lent itself to a deep firebox between the coupled axles which was easy to fire and could be pushed to high outputs without unduly pulling the fire about.

The rival 4-4-2 "Atlantic" was always the preferred choice of a few railways only, from Ivatt's 1898 "Klondykes" for the GNR to Marsh's H2s of 1911 for the LB&SCR. As more power was demanded the usual successor to the 4-4-0 was a 4-6-0, though the transition went through difficult birth pangs until the right formula was recognised.

Both the 4-4-0 and 4-4-2 lasted well into BR days. At the hand-over to British Railways on 1st January 1948 no less than 1615 4-4-0s were included. The GWR contribution was small, but on the LMS and LNER they amounted to about 8% of their fleets and from the Southern a massive 20%; substantial numbers of the latter were still hard at it on top link expresses. Elsewhere their work was almost entirely secondary after being cascaded downwards as new and larger locomotives took their places in the front line.

If the 1920s still gave the railways a cosy corner of the travel market with only limited competition, the 1930s saw a change of scene with increasing demands for higher sustained speeds with steadily growing loads as passenger amenity was improved. This development seems to have been inadequately foreseen by the railways; up to the end of 1932 the four companies provided six designs of 4-4-0 (the seventh, the SR 'Schools', was in a class of its own) which were never going to be masters of the evolving requirements. Why?

On the LMS the Midland influence of the first eight years led to 195 class 4P compounds and 138 class 2P simple 4-4-0s being built, representing blind adherence to small trains and plenty of them. But that thinking was never going to succeed on the West Coast route, even before accelerations started in earnest in 1932. Double headed trains on all sides? Sir Josiah Stamp, the President and an economist, was not going to accept *that*. The compounds quickly gravitated to stopping passenger and piloting work. Maybe the answer at that time would have been Fowler's 1924 project of a three cylinder compound 4-6-0.

And the class 2Ps? At least they showed some improvement over their Midland ancestors, but their scope was very limited. The Somerset & Dorset? No way could the summer Bournemouth traffic be limited to their permitted 200 tons. The Stranraer road? No doubt *some* trains could be held down to their 170 tons capability. But you have only to look at the allocation outside the G&SW section; two here, three there, for branch work or the engineer's saloon. Every shed should have a couple, they are going begging!

On the other side of the country, 24 "Directors" and (ultimately) 76 three cylinder D49s were bought by the LNER. The "Directors" one could excuse; in 1924 power was wanted for Scotland in a hurry and these engines could really run trains. They proved it by continuing to work many of the Great Central expresses until 1936, when the "Sandringhams" arrived in force. But the D49s, specially built for secondary expresses? Much of the intended work was either easy or beyond them single-handed. Perhaps a lesser influx of B17s to North East England and Scotland would have made better sense; if you could keep the Great Central's sharp timings over a hard road with ten bogies on your tail, there would not be much elsewhere that was beyond a B17 to perform.

One can skate over Swindon's aberration with the thirty little "Dukedog" museum pieces; they were assembled from sound parts of withdrawn and obsolete engines in 1936. Perhaps the powers that be were dazzled by the length of the first nameplate *Earl of Mount Edgcumbe* which took up the whole circumference of the splasher, they found a little niche pottering about the Cambrian lines where life was not lived at a frenetic pace.

On the Southern, new construction was severely constrained. Much of the Eastern Section was barred to anything bigger than moderate sized 4-4-0s for some years by engineering restrictions, and Maunsell's fifteen L1s of 1926 were designed within those limits, following the splendid superheated D1s and E1s. But it was the forty "Schools" from 1930 which were the masterpieces, squeezed to get through the undersized tunnels of the Tonbridge-Hastings line yet getting Class 5 power out of a 4-4-0 by using three "Lord Nelson" cylinders and a shortened "King Arthur" boiler. An unconventional solution perhaps, but it was to prove itself beyond all expectations later on other routes as well, notably the Portsmouth Direct, and to Dover and Bournemouth. So one might be pilloried for suggesting that the 'Schools' design might not have been ideal outside the Hastings line, but for the Dover boat trains, and the Bournemouth Belle, it is arguable that more "King Arthurs" might have been a better overall proposition.

A real *multum in parvo* machine, the 4-4-0. No wonder that enthusiasts still make pilgrimages to Pakistan to see the last survivors of the breed.   AJP

Table 2 summarises all the 4-4-0 types received by BR on 1st January 1948 and the subsequent totals at the beginning of each year down to 1963. In July of that year, the 4-4-0 finally disappeared from BR with the withdrawal of LSWR T9 No. 120. As we have already stated, there were so many overall that it is impossible to deal with them all within the confines of one book and this, the first of two volumes, takes a countrywide look at specific classes. Volume Two will be complimentary, working on the same theme for the remaining classes.

Type Origin and Class	TITLE 2: 4-4-0 locomotives taken into BR stock on 1st January 1948. Note: Classes marked * are illustrated in this volume; the remainder will appear in the sequel.															
	1948	1949	1950	1951	1952	1953	1954	1955	1956	1957	1958	1959	1960	1961	1962	1963
LMS AND CONSTITUENTS																
MR 2P 6'6"	3	3	1	1	1											
MR 2P 7' 0"	157	153	137	124	112	98	86	77	69	59	41	34	22	16	3	
SDJR 2P "322"	5	5	5	4	4	4	2	2	2							
LMS 2P (Three ex-SDJR)	136	136	136	136	136	136	136	135	135	135	134	134	91	81	15	
MR 3P	22	17	10	8	3											
MR 4P Compound*	45	37	32	28	11	1										
LMS 4P Compound*	195	195	195	195	195	189	176	153	116	89	55	19	6	2		
LNWR Precursor* (superheated)	1	1														
LNWR George the Fifth*	3															
CR "900" Dunalastair III 3P (superheated)	1															
CR "140" Dunalastair IV 2P	1															
CR Dunalastair IV 3P (superheated "140", "139" and "43")	22	22	22	22	22	21	18	16	7	7	1					
CR "113/928" Pickersgill 3P	16	16	16	16	16	16	16	16	16	16	16	16	7	7	1	
CR "72" Pickersgill 3P	32	32	32	32	32	32	31	31	31	31	31	31	24	18	5	
HR Loch 2P	2	1	1													
HR Small Ben 2P	10	7	4	2	2	1										
LNER AND CONSTITUENTS																
GNR D1	7	5	4													
GNR D2	31	21	6	1												
GNR D3	19	13	5	1												
GCR D9*	26	26	7													
GCR D10*	10	10	10	10	10	10	6	3								
GCR D11/1*	11	11	11	11	11	11	11	11	11	11	11	11	10			
GCR D11/2*	24	24	24	24	24	24	24	24	24	24	24	22	14	14	1	
GER D15*	13	12	12	10	5											
GER D16/2*	16	10	4	3	1											
GER D16/3*	88	89	94	94	94	92	90	90	75	67	39	17	4			
NER D17/2	2															
NER D20 (includes 3 D20/2)	50	48	47	47	28	28	27	17	14	7						

Type Origin and Class	Note: Classes marked * are illustrated in this volume; the remainder will appear in the sequel.															
	1948	1949	1950	1951	1952	1953	1954	1955	1956	1957	1958	1959	1960	1961	1962	1963
NBR D29*	12	9	5	3	2											
NBR D30*	25	25	25	25	24	24	24	24	24	24	16	6	2			
NBR D31*	7	4	3	2	1											
NBR D32*	10	2	1	1												
NBR D33*	10	9	7	7	3	1										
NBR D34* (‡ No. 256 *Glen Douglas* wdn 12-62)	30	30	28	27	27	27	27	27	27	27	27	26	14	6	1‡	
GNSR D40 (‡ No. 49 *Gordon Highlander* wdn 6-58)	18	18	18	18	18	18	15	15	6	2	1‡					
GNSR D41	22	21	19	16	9	3										
LNER D49/1* (‡includes 2 withdrawn 1-1-60)	34	34	34	34	34	34	34	34	34	34	32	22	12‡	9		
LNER D49/2*	41	41	41	41	41	41	41	41	41	41	36	16	10	5		
LNER D* (Thompson rebuild of 62768)	1	1	1	1	1											
GWR DESIGNS																
GWR Duke	11	11	4	2												
GWR Bulldog*	45	28	9	8												
GWR 9000	29	26	26	26	26	26	26	24	22	22	8	6	5			
SOUTHERN AND CONSTITUENTS																
LSWR T9 (‡No. 120 repainted, remained in BR stock until July 1963)	66	66	66	66	46	38	37	36	36	35	31	24	14	13	1‡	1‡
LSWR K10	31	23	8	2												
LSWR L11	40	40	34	28	6											
LSWR S11	10	10	10	10	1	1	1									
LSWR L12	20	20	20	20	2	2	1	1								
LSWR D15	10	10	10	10	8	4	4	2	1							
SER F1*	9	4														
SER B1*	16	9	3	1												
SECR D*	28	28	28	27	18	18	13	10	6							
SECR E*	15	15	15	15	3	3	2	1								
SECR L*	22	22	22	22	22	22	22	22	22	20	20	18	10	8		
SECR D1*	20	20	20	19	17	17	17	17	17	17	17	17	15	11		
SECR E1*	11	11	10	8	7	7	7	7	7	7	7	5	4	3		
SR L1*	15	15	15	15	15	15	15	15	15	15	15	15	13	10	1	
LBSCR B4	7	6	5	4												
LBSCR B4X	12	12	12	12												
SR Schools	40	40	40	40	40	40	40	40	40	40	40	40	40	40	25	

This list does not include service locomotives. Several locomotives were restored to pre Grouping liveries and numbers and ran mostly special trains e.g. LSWR No. 120, NBR No. 256 and GNSR No. 49 (withdrawn before repainting), these are included up to their withdrawal from capital stock. However some continued to run on BR after these dates. No. 3440 *City of Truro*, and MR No. 1000 have not been included as they had been withdrawn and later restored to working order, although No. 3440 was reinstated to Western Region stock, on loan from the old York Museum, between January 1957 and May 1961.

The Midland/LMS Compounds

The LMS inherited 45 Compounds from the Midland and 195 were built in the Company's early years (at Derby and Horwich, together with outside contractors North British Locomotive Co. and Vulcan Foundry) as stop gap main line express engines, working trains not only over the Midland route but also the West Coast Main Line and such trains as the London to Birmingham two hour expresses.

They were Britain's most numerous 4-4-0 design and the largest class of 3-cylinder compounds anywhere in the world. The Midland engines dated from Johnson and Deeley's time and all were eventually rebuilt with superheaters into the form which the LMS-built examples displayed from new. Although they were a highly successful design, their lack of absolute size made them unsuitable for the very heaviest of LMS trains, but they were spread over the major part of the LMS system.

The last passenger train hauled by a Compound in regular service was the 9.05 am Sheffield Midland-Derby slow on Sunday 21st August 1960. By Nationalisation these were the only compound locomotives working on the system and by the date of withdrawal of the last engine (No. 41168 from Monument Lane, Birmingham in July 1961) their life span had covered almost sixty years since the original Johnson Compound had taken to the rails in 1902. The latter engine was, quite properly, preserved (in rebuilt and superheated form) in the National Collection.

Above: Midland Compound, BR No. 41009, one of eight allocated to Bedford shed (15D), is seen at the head of the 6.52 pm St. Pancras-Bedford local near Radlett on 24th July 1950. The stock is composed of LMS standard non-corridor coaches which seated 6 a side in the third class in comparative comfort. No. 41009 was built at Derby in December 1905 as No. 1004 renumbered 1009 in 1907, and was super-heated in 1922. Withdrawal came some 16 months after this photograph was taken, in December 1951. The locomotive livery is an early BR hybrid of LNWR lined black with British Railways in full on the tender. The tender itself is the original Deeley Midland type, built new for this class of locomotive and which more or less set the style for the later MR/LMS standard 3500 gallon type. (E. D. Bruton/NRM)

Left: Midland built Compound No. 41028 (6/06-10/52) of Bristol Barrow Road (22A) rounds the curve at Mangotsfield North Junction (the photograph was taken from the signalbox) with a Bristol-Gloucester local in 1952. Once again the tender is interesting: this time it is an LMS standard tank (designed to fit a 13ft wheelbase chassis) mounted onto a still serviceable ex-MR 15ft wheelbase underframe, thus giving rise to a wide platform at the rear of the tender body. The train consists of three Stanier corridors with a non corridor third of LNWR origin leading.

The lines from Bath join from the left and the imposing building in the background is Carson's chocolate factory. Mangotsfield North Junction was the site of the original MR station closed in 1869 although goods facilities remained here. The Midland built Compounds were withdrawn by January 1953 but LMS examples were allocated to Gloucester and Bristol to replace them.

Right: Two LMS built Compounds head the 2.00 pm Birmingham to Barnt Green, Bromsgrove and Worcester on 12th May 1949. This was a regular double headed turn and the second engine is possibly No. 41047 (2/24-2/54) of Gloucester shed (22B) which was also a frequent performer. No. 41046 (2/24-1/53), of Saltley (21A), has the original low cut frames which were susceptible to buckling – a hard bang would do it! This view also shows quite clearly the somewhat unusual arrangement whereby the connecting rod from the cylinders to the driving wheel was fixed *inside* the coupling rods. This reversal of customary practice was a characteristic feature of the compounds and enabled the cylinders to be set slightly further 'inboard' than would otherwise have been possible.

The exhaust injector steam pipe has been added on the fireman's side and the tender rivets show that a new tank has been fitted – again to a former MR chassis of larger wheelbase. An unusual feature is the blanking off of the washout plugs. Note the dreadful condition of the station roof – arising from bomb damage in World War II probably in 1940/41. (P. B. Whitehouse/Millbrook House Collection)

Left: The up Thames-Clyde express leaving Leeds City (Midland side) double headed c. 1951/2. The pilot is Compound No. 41096 of Nottingham (16A) which may have been working home. The train engine is a Jubilee. No. 1096 was built at Derby in August 1925 (left hand drive) and withdrawn in April 1954. (Eric Treacy/Millbrook House Collection)

Below: Compound No. 41104 (10/25-8/55) of Leeds Holbeck shed (20A) standing in the loco yard at Leeds City (formerly Wellington) c.1952 (No. 41104 was transferred to Holbeck in August 1952). Note the Midland water column with 'swan neck' and the 50ft hand operated turntable. The tender No. 2764 is yet another 3500 gallon LMS standard body sans beading on a Midland long frame and appears to be anonymous! (Eric Treacy/ Millbrook House Collection)

Opposite: Sheffield and Midland Joint. Compound No. 41066 of Trafford Park (9E) on a down local to Manchester Central approaching Romiley in 1952. Before the opening of the Midland direct line via Cheadle Heath in 1902 the MR access to Manchester was over lines jointly owned by the Midland and Manchester Sheffield & Lincolnshire and some local trains continued to use this route until the closure of Manchester Central in 1969. No. 41066 was built at Derby in August 1924 (an LMS right hand drive example) and withdrawn in May 1958.

The carriages are of Stanier LMS design but note that the side panelling of the second vehicle (a brake third) partly hides the upper part of the underframe – an indication that this carriage had a welded underframe to which the body panels were fixed direct (ie without a separate bottom horizontal frame member). (Millbrook House Collection)

Right: LMS Compound No. 41111 (11/25-5/58) heads the 10.00 am Rhyl-Chester all stations local through the sandstone cutting (note the vertical unlined walls) at the approaches to Chester on 21st August 1951. The stock is period I LMS lavatory non-corridors (ie wood-panelled with raised beading). The chimney is the tall Stanier type and there is a blue spot marking above the number to indicate that the locomotive is prohibited from travelling over certain lines, particularly the Scottish routes of the old LMS. Once again the tender is 'hybrid' – almost certainly replacing the original Midland tender with which this engine (in spite of its LMS Standard origin) was long paired in pre-BR days. (P. M. Alexander/Millbrook House Collection)

Left: The Midland side of Birmingham New Street station c.1955 with two LMS class 4P Compound 4-4-0s. On the right at Platform 7, No. 40932 is about to depart on the 1.45 pm to Yarmouth Beach via the Midland & Great Northern Joint line and running into Platform 8 is No. 40928 with the 11.30 local from Gloucester due at 1.48 pm. The Yarmouth must have been a few minutes late departing. The leading carriage behind No. 40932 is an LMS design corridor composite with 'Porthole' windows, a type not actually built until BR days. It had an integral steel welded body and welded chassis and formed a sort of 'halfway house' to the BR Mk I type. The station itself is looking very tatty after war damage and years of neglect but another 12 years were to pass before rebuilding was completed. Both locomotives were built by the Vulcan Foundry at Newton-le-Willows in May 1927. No. 40928 was withdrawn in March 1958 and 40932 in May 1956. The allocation of the locomotives during the summer of 1955 was: Saltley (21A): No. 40928 and Gloucester Barnwood (22B): No. 40932. (A. W. Flowers)

The LNWR 'Precursors' and 'Georges'

When George Whale took over the post of Chief Mechanical Engineer in 1903 he set about revolutionising the LNWR motive power and his 'Precursor' class was widely acclaimed. This was followed in 1910 by the famous 'George the Fifth' 4-4-0s of C. J. Bowen Cooke, Schmidt-superheated and leaders in their field: together with the 'Claughton' 4-6-0s they headed the Premier Line's major expresses to the end of its days and well into the LMS period.

In due time many, but by no means all of the 'Precursors' were superheated making them virtually indistinguishable in performance from the 'George the Fifths' and in appearance too, save for the older splasher design. They were displaced from their duties by the new Stanier classes and would all have been scrapped by the early 1940s had it not been for World War II. They were magnificent engines, perhaps the finest ever built with two inside cylinders, being well capable of handling trains of 400 tons. Only one superheated 'Precursor', No. 25297 *Sirocco* and three 'Georges' Nos. 25321 *Lord Loch,* 25350 (once *India)* and 25373 *Ptarmigan* came into BR stock. None carried BR numbers and, very regrettably, none were preserved.

Above: The last of the 'Georges'. No. 25350 (6/11-5/48), named *India* until this name was applied to Stanier Jubilee No. 5574 in 1936, takes water at Llandudno servicing point before working back to her home depot at Chester with a return summer Saturday express. The chalk letters RSD 929 on the smokebox door refer to the code for Rolling Stock Distribution; the headlamp code shows that of an empty stock train. Note the Belpaire boiler, modified cab and (probably) an ex-'Claughton' tender. (Millbrook House Collection)

Above and below: Like most of her clan No. 25297 *Sirocco* (11/04-6/49) ended her days at Chester shed (6A) usually working North Wales coast semi-fasts and relief expresses though occasionally wandering down the branch to Denbigh. These pictures were taken on Chester shed in the summer of 1948. By now, the engine had received a Belpaire boiler (basically an LMS period modification) and a rounded cab roof shape – again an LMS modification (applied to many ex-LNWR engines), designed to allow the locomotives so altered to clear the LMS 'composite' loading gauge. The tender is also interesting. It is not the original Whale type but the final Bowen Cooke design with fabricated top coping and 'sausage'-shaped frame slots – almost certainly 'rescued' from a withdrawn 'Claughton' 4-6-0. (P. B. Whitehouse/Millbrook House Collection)

Above: Technically a few months before the period covered by this book 'George the Fifth' Class 4-4-0 No. 25350 takes the 3.50 pm from Bangor to Birmingham out of Llandudno Junction on Whit Monday 1947. This was a heavy train made up to thirteen coaches, seemingly mostly of LNWR origin – a very typical load for a 'George' in its prime but somewhat less common at this time.

At this date, the engine still displayed the original pattern of LNWR 'round top' boiler and it was by no means unusual (given the frequency of boiler changing during heavy repairs) for the same engine to alternate between Belpaire and round top as the years passed by. But Belpaire boxes were all but universal at the very end. (P. B. Whitehouse/Millbrook House Collection)

Below: All the LNWR 4-4-0s had gravitated to Chester shed (6A) by Nationalisation. No. 25321 *Lord Loch,* disfigured by a Stanier chimney (the only 'George' to be so fitted, though No. 25304 *Greyhound* a superheated 'Precursor' suffered likewise), heads the 6.20 pm Chester-Corwen on Whit Monday 1947. It is running late and crossing the 5.50 pm Denbigh to Chester hauled by a Stanier 2-6-4 tank, at Broughton & Bretton. (P. B. Whitehouse/Millbrook House Collection)

Robinson's Great Central Contribution

The LNER passed on 71 GCR 4-4-0s, all of Robinson design, in 1948. The three classes (D9, D10 and D11) were all built for express passenger work, the D11 type eclipsing both 4-4-2 and 4-6-0 designs over the difficult GC main line. Problems with lack of investment on the NBR system in the days prior to Grouping persuaded Gresley to order 24 more D11s (only 11 were built by the GCR) for Scotland; no doubt Robinson's role as locomotive consultant assisted the choice. Other than conforming to the NBR loading gauge, the D11/2s built in 1924 were almost identical to the GCR types.

By Nationalisation, Thompson B1 4-6-0s, already 274 in number, were being delivered at a rate of over two per week confining the D11s (like so many other LNER 4-4-0s) to secondary duties. However despite long periods in store they were still competent performers and lasted until 1960 in England and, north of the border, just into 1962.

The Cheshire Lines Committee witnessed the demise of the D9 and D10 classes, although both worked expresses right up to the end.

Opposite: The ex Great Central Railway Robinson D9's career under BR ownership was brief. The twenty six members of the class taken over had all disappeared by July 1950 having spent their last days working the Cheshire Lines routes. In this view, the last of the D9s No. 62305 (2/02-7/50) leaves Mouldsworth at 9.02 am with a Chester-Manchester train on 10th May 1949. A junction with tracks from the Birkenhead Joint at Helsby, by now freight only, came in on the far side of the overbridge opposite the signal box (just visible). No. 62305 spent its final days at Trafford Park shed (9E).

Right: D9 No. 62311 (3/02-7/49) at Manchester Central with an express probably for Southport on 7th May 1949. Express headlamps not withstanding, the train itself is of non-corridor stock! The D9s were now past their prime and the LMR take over of the CLC motive power in November 1948 spelt the end. No. 62311 was allocated to Walton on the Hill depot in Liverpool, from where it was withdrawn. Also in shot is Darnall based B1 4-6-0 No. 61153 (5/47-1/65); their introduction on the Manchester-Sheffield section allowed the Sheffield based D10s to be moved onto CLC services.

Left: Through the heart of Delamere Forest. Class D9 No. 62330, a Vulcan Foundry engine, (4/04-8/49) takes a morning Chester-Manchester express up the 1:90 from Mouldsworth on the 10th May 1949. It is fitted with a low dome cover and later pattern LNER chimney. Like a number of her sisters No. 62330 is a Northwich engine. The train is a fairly characteristic CLC mixture. Most of the vehicles are of GCR pattern in a combination of high and low roof styles, but the second vehicle is clearly a Doncaster product with GNR styling. Though jointly owned by the GCR, GNR and MR, only the first two of these companies provided passenger coaches for the CLC – almost always in the then current style of the parent company, but marked, of course, for the CLC itself. (P. M. Alexander/Millbrook House Collection–all)

Above: D10 No. 62650 *Prince Henry* (8/13-2/54) passes Chester South Box with the 6.44 Chester Northgate-Manchester Central service on 10th May 1949. Note the Great Central pattern signal controlling the junction with the GCR branch to Bidston. It was around this time that the class was concentrated west of the Pennines of CLC duties, No. 62650 being allocated to Northwich shed. The carriages visible are some of the spacious high-roofed non-corridors to GCR design and style. (P. M. Alexander/Millbrook House Collection)

Right: The last D10, No. 62653 *Sir Edward Fraser* (10/13-10/55), stands at the servicing point outside Manchester Central station (just visible on the left) on 7th May 1949. It received its BR number in 1948 (prior to the adoption of the tender emblem) and was, therefore lettered "British Railways" in full. There is a glass sight screen fitted just ahead of the cab cut out. These features were sometimes known as 'cinder guards' – a clear reference to their value in protecting the eyes of the footplate crew when they needed to lean out of the cab. No. 62653 was a Liverpool Brunswick engine at the time although like most of the class it ended its days working stopping passenger diagrams from Northwich shed. (P. M. Alexander/Millbrook House Collection)

Above: D11/1 No. 62663 *Prince Albert* (3/20-5/60) heads south out of York past Holgate with an afternoon Sheffield express in the summer of 1957. By this time the D11/1s were in a thoroughly run down condition, spending long periods in store, and only occasionally seen on summer express services. However this hide and seek existence was to continue until 1960 when the majority of the class was withdrawn, the last, No. 62666, going in December. No. 62663 was a Sheffield Darnall (41A) engine and on transfer to Staveley in 1958 spent its last days working local passenger trains. The train is a mixture of LNE and LMS stock headed by a post war Thompson full brake with deal-boarded flat sides. Travellers on this train would scarcely believe, let alone recognise the modern highly simplified track layout now to be seen at Holgate Bridge in consequence of the ECML electrification work during 1989. (Eric Treacy/Millbrook House Collection)

Above: The cab interior of Robinson's Improved Director class (LNER class D11/1) eleven of which were built at Gorton between 1919 and 1922. All the Director series of engines were right hand drive including those built for Scotland in 1924, even though the NBR had latterly adopted the left hand position. In 1925 the LNER also chose the left hand drive standard. The Scottish Directors had a lower cab roof and straight front windows. Note how high the firehole is up the backplate, a position not designed to make the fireman's job any easier and not welcomed in Scotland! (Millbrook House Collection)

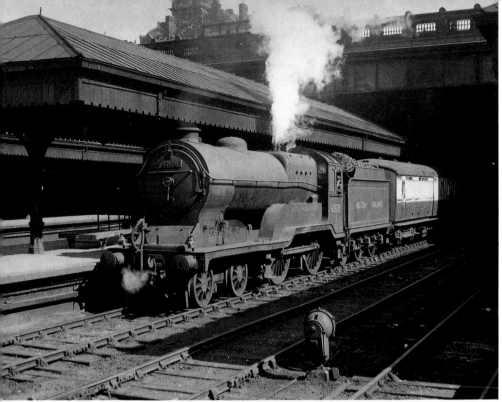

Left: D11/2 No. 62678 *Luckie Mucklebackit* (9/24-3/59) of 64B Haymarket shed leaves the west end of Endinburgh Waverley at 12.18 with an express for Dundee in the early 1950s. The lower boiler mountings and cab roof (to suit the NBR loading gauge) of the LNER Scottish 'Directors' are clearly visible. The locomotive is fitted with LNER Group Standard buffers rather than GCR oval pattern and retains the wheel and handle smokebox door fastening.

The painted names of the Scottish 'Directors' were a distinctive feature of these robust locomotives, both in LNER and BR days and the chosen names were a wonderfully resonant collection of appropriately Scottish origin. In fact the painting of names on Scottish-based or Scottish-owned locomotives was by far the most common method of naming engines north of the border; nameplates as such were rather rare. It was therefore a thoughtful gesture on Gresley's part to continue this tradition with the D11/2s after the grouping. (Eric Treacy/Millbrook House Collection)

Right: Armstrong Whitworth built D11/2 No. 62686 *The Fiery Cross* (10/24-7/61) runs through Dalmeny at the head of a Dundee-Edinburgh train in July 1948 just after receiving the prefix 6 to its post war LNER number. The locomotive is in apple green with Gill Sans lettering and allocated to Eastfield with the depot name painted on the bufferbeam in the late LNER style. Once again, the painted name is characteristic. The train itself is more than normally interesting, being composed mainly of ex-GNR and early LNER standard gangwayed coaches with an ex-NER non corridor third leading – and probably added as a 'strengthener'. It was an interesting feature of the Scottish scene (both on the former LNER and former LMS lines) that many erstwhile English carriages ended their days north of the border; and the use of ex-NER stock on former NBR lines was particularly common. (P. M. Alexander/Millbrook House Collection)

Great Eastern Survivors

The 'Claud Hamilton' 4-4-0s turned out from Stratford works in 1900 in deep blue livery with copper capped chimneys must have been a delight to behold. They worked the principal expresses out of Liverpool Street to Norwich and the East Coast side by side with the equally smart and successful 4-6-0s (built from 1911), later LNER Class B12. The 4-4-0 design went through a continuous process of evolution through the GER, LNER and even BR periods. The final product (Class D16/3), rebuilt with long travel piston valves and a Gresley round top boiler at the instigation of Thompson, was the most numerous at Nationalisation and conversions continued until 1949.

They remained on main line duties until replaced by the Gresley 'Sandringham' 3 cylinder 4-6-0s, the Thompson B1 4-6-0s and latterly the 'Britannias'. Many then went on to find work elsewhere, over the M&GN, the Cheshire Lines Committee, the Cambridge-Oxford line and over a large part of the LMR system in the East Midlands. However East Anglia remained their stronghold, where they continued working secondary expresses (as well as locals in Norfolk and Suffolk) until 1960, when more modern engines were available – displaced by the tide of dieselisation, electrification (particularly the Southend Victoria services from 31-12-56) and route closures.

Above: South Lynn (31D) based class D15/2 No. 62507 (6/00-4/52) was one of the first batch of 11 'Claud Hamilton' 4-4-0s built at Stratford in 1900. It is being turned at Kings Lynn shed in June 1951. Note the 'watercart' tender. This, combined with the extended smokebox and removal of the valancing, certainly detracted from the appearance of a type normally noted for its pleasing lines. The older 'Clauds' were drafted onto the M&GN to help replace the Midland style 4-4-0s, the last of which were withdrawn in January 1945. (Millbrook House Collection)

Above: Melton Constable (32G) based D15 No. 62538 (10/03-4/52) arrives at its home town with the daily goods from Cromer around noon on 23rd May 1951. This was the only D15 to receive BR lined black livery. It is fitted with twin anti-vacuum valves behind a GNR style chimney. Also note the M&GN somersault signals, mounted on a concrete post. The GER 4-4-0s were unusual in having their front guard irons attached in front of the bufferbeam. (P. M. Alexander/Millbrook House Collection)

Left: Only four D16s were withdrawn as Belpaire boilered D16/2s; these included No. 62603 (3/11-9/51) of March shed seen here leaving Bury St. Edmunds with a southbound express in August 1949. Note the GER chimney and the three road shed just visible in the background. One of the two rather incongruous Baroque towers which dominate the station area appears behind the engine's tender.

The leading carriage is of NER design – a reminder of the fact that soon after the grouping, the NER standard 53ft 6in corridor coach design was adopted by Gresley for the GE section, since it was not possible to accept the larger (61ft 6in) LNER standard carriages on much of the former GE territory. Later, Gresley introduced a shorter 52ft 6in version of the LNER standard type for use in East Anglia. (P. M. Alexander/Millbrook House Collection)

Right: D16/3 No. 62536 (9/03-7/55) leaves Marks Tey at 6.40 pm with a through Ipswich-Cambridge train on Saturday 18th June 1949. A North Eastern clerestory heads the rake. In 1950 this engine was one of eight 'Clauds' transferred to Trafford Park shed (by then part of the LMR) to work the CLC expresses, due to the crews' dislike of the ex-LMS Class 2Ps and more especially the ex-LMS compounds. In October 1952, No. 62536 was on the move again, this time to the ex-Midland depot at Peterborough Spital Bridge (35B) working trains to Rugby, Leicester and Northampton; when the B12/3s took over these services in July 1955 No. 62536 was withdrawn. (P. M. Alexander/Millbrook House Collection)

Right: A clean, but unlined, black D16/3 No. 62540 (11/03-8/59) rounds the curve, off the Dereham line, at Wymondham South Junction into the station with an (East) Dereham-Norwich train on Wednesday 23rd May 1951. The shed plate reads 32A, Norwich. Note disc headcodes are still in use on the Great Eastern section.

   The neatly manicured bullhead track and the spacious nature of the associated sidings (none of which have been lifted) give a timeless quality to the scene which, locomotive and train livery apart, had probably not changed in essence for a generation or more. (P. M. Alexander/Millbrook House Collection)

Below: During the first two years of Nationalisation twelve D16/2s were converted to round top boilered D16/3s; No. 62577 was one such. Built in December 1909 as a saturated (LNER class D15) engine, in May 1949 it was converted from D16/2 to D16/3 and withdrawn in October 1956. The Norwich (32A) based locomotive is seen here leaving Wells-next-the-Sea (Wells on Sea is displayed on the signalbox) with a local train for Heacham in April 1952.

   The stock is also very interesting, the leading vehicle is to a North Eastern design, with Gresley bogies, built just after Grouping. It was Westinghouse brake fitted and on a short underframe suitable for the GE section as well as being a more modern design. Behind is an open third articulated twin set of Gresley's tourist stock. Originally (pre-war) painted green and cream, this pair of carriages are probably now still wearing their drab wartime (and afterwards) brown livery. Note the lower quandrant semaphores set at an angle to allow sighting round the very sharp curve. (P. B. Whitehouse/Millbrook House Collection)

Above: Kings Lynn bustles with activity in this mid 1950s view taken from the Tennyson Avenue crossing footbridge as D16/3 No. 62601 (2/11-1/57) departs with an express for Liverpool Street. The lines to the right on which J17 No. 65568 (5/05-9/58) is shunting (it carries white and red lamps) lead to the goods depot and docks. Behind No. 62601 is Kings Lynn shed (31C) its home depot; two 'Clauds' are visible including No. 62530 (5/02-9/58) whilst a further GER type is lifted on the sheerlegs undergoing repair. Two GNR C12 4-4-2 tanks are also on shed. (P. J. Lynch)

Left: A Royal engine: Class D16/3 No. 62618 resplendent in fully lined apple green, with the first BR symbol (a very rare combination) heads a Cambridge train out of Colchester in the summer of 1950 or 1951. One of the last series of 'Clauds' built at Stratford by the LNER in 1923 it retained the decorative valancing when converted to a D16/3 in 1944. The locomotive was repainted apple green by BR in October 1949 and carried the livery for two years. This engine was based at Cambridge (31A), whilst the other 'Royal Claud' BR No. 62614 was kept at Kings Lynn (31C). The GE section was probably the last area on BR to retain specifically 'dedicated' Royal Train locomotives. (Millbrook House Collection)

Below: The last 'Claud', D16/3 No. 62613, was built at Stratford in 1923 (first LNER No. 8782) and was finally withdrawn from March (31B) shed in October 1960. It spent the summer months working mostly local passenger services as required. In this view, the engine passes Whitemoor Junction with the 9.24 am March-Kings Lynn train on 4th June 1960. Note the GWR horse box followed by BR built General Utility Van and later BR symbol on the tender. (W. J. Probert/ Millbrook House Collection)

The 'Scottish School' – NBR Style

As with most of its pre Grouping constituents the LNER inherited a large number of 4-4-0s from the North British Railway, 183 engines in all. Twenty five years later at Nationalisation the LNER handed on 51% of these engines (only the GER 4-4-0s bettered this with 62%) forming two distinct types, the 6ft Intermediates designed for mixed traffic work and the 6ft 6in passenger engines. Most were now confined to secondary duties or branch line working, although the 'Glens' continued to double head the West Highland trains with the K2 Moguls for the first few years. The introduction of the Thompson B1s, Peppercorn K1s and finally the Stanier Black Fives sounded the death knell and by the late 1950s and early 1960s they were redundant.

The NBR 4-4-0 locomotives represent the first view in this survey of those characteristic products of what has become known as the 'Scottish School'. This was a style of locomotive which, we guess, derived much of its characteristic form from the early work of such eminent men as William Stroudley and Dugald Drummond. They had many disciples and followers and we shall meet them again in the sequel volume in the context of the Caledonian and Highland 4-4-0s in Scotland and some of the surviving LSWR 4-4-0s in England. They were truly distinctive designs; none more so than those of the NBR whose survivors to BR dated from the time of Matthew Holmes and W. P. Reid. It was W. P. Reid who re-introduced the practice of naming engines on the NBR in 1906, and most of his subsequent 'passenger' types were thus adorned.

Above: Twelve of the original sixteen 'Scott' Class D29s (designed by Reid) survived into Nationalisation although, as with so many of the LNER 4-4-0 classes, the flood of Thompson 4-6-0s in the late 1040s and early 1950s quickly consigned them to the scrap heap. The final example proved to an an unusual one in several respects. No. 62411 *Lady of Avenel* (11/11-11/52) was repainted in post war apple green in September 1947 a livery which it carried until withdrawal (note the patch of paint applied in order to renumber into the BR series and the power classification 3P). It was the only NBR 4-4-0 to receive this livery. Also of interest is the extended smokebox fitted only to No. 62411 in an attempt to prevent the all too common occurance of burnt smokebox doors. The loco is at its home depot Thornton Junction (62A) on 13th April 1952 where it was employed on local passenger services in Fife. Behind, sporting dumb buffers, is former NBR Class J88 0-6-0T No. 68323 (12/04-10/56) one of a class of dock shunters which lasted until December 1962. (A. G. Ellis/Colour Rail)

Right: More typical of the original 'Scott' Class (with normal smokebox), No. 62412 *Dirk Hatteraick* (12/11-9/50) is seen in remarkably clean condition c.1949 at Wormit, heading a local train, tender-first, towards Newport and Tayport (a branch long closed). The D29s started life as the saturated fore-runners of the later (and superheated) D30 Class but, even though the NBR classified them both as 'J' and the D29s were later superheated, the LNER based its classification on their original condition. The circular spectacle plate windows on the D29s always differentiated them from their D30 successors. No. 62412 is seen here in the newly applied BR lined black livery before the adoption of the first BR tender emblem. (Gavin Wilson/Atlantic Collection)

Below: A later NBR 'Scott' (LNER D30/2) – note the changed cab spectacle window shape – runs into North Queensferry with a southbound local on 14th July 1951. No. 62431 *Kenilworth* built in October 1914 looks to be in poor condition but worked out of Thornton Junction (62A) for another seven years until its withdrawal in October 1958. The smokebox door has become distorted allowing air to leak in and burn the door. (J. Robertson/Colour Rail)

Hawick shed (64G) had an allocation of eight D30s through much of the fifties including the appropriately named *Wandering Willie* No. 62440 (11/20-7/58) seen here on shed early in the decade. In the goods sidings behind is D49/1 No. 62719 *Peebles-shire* (5/28-1/60) attached to a GCR tender. Also in view is a military train conveying mostly brengun carriers. Hawick was a stone built two road shed with an allocation of 22 locomotives in April 1954. Its D30s were employed on passenger services to Edinburgh and (via Riccarton Junction and Hexham) to Newcastle. The shed also supplied locomotives for banking duties up the 10½ mile climb to Whitrope summit, No. 62440 is probably awaiting such a turn. (Eric Treacy/Millbrook House Collection)

Seven of these Holmes 6ft 6in engines (LNER class D31) were taken over by BR, the oldest No. 2059 (5/90-12/52) proving to be the longest lived. In 1949 the building of the K1 2-6-0s created a clash of numbers with those allocated to the D31s in 1946, thus in August No. 62059 became No. 62281. The locomotive still retains its Westinghouse brake equipment which was removed from other classes of NBR 4-4-0 in the 1930s, the D31s were candidates for early withdrawal even then! No. 62281 is seen at its home depot, Carlisle Canal (68E), on 20th August 1952. Apart from shunting coal wagons the loco worked passenger services on the Silloth branch and very occasionally over the Waverley route. Behind is the wagon tippler of the mechanical coaling plant, built in the 1930s, showing the underframe of a standard RCH mineral wagon. The shed catered for an allocation of around 60 locomotives at this period. (J. Robertson/Colour Rail)

The Reid class D32 4-4-0s (in effect, small-wheeled 'Scotts') were already over forty years old by 1948 and two of the twelve built had been withdrawn at the end of 1947. All ten inherited by BR retained LNER plain black livery and only one (the last withdrawn in March 1951) No. 2451 received a BR number. No. 2444 (11/06-9/48) stands in the dismal surroundings of St. Margarets shed around 1947, with wartime abbreviation NE on the tender. The St. Margarets D32s were employed on a variety of local duties including assisting trains from Dunbar, a task later performed by 'Glens' and on empty stock to and from Craigentinny. No. 2445 latterly worked the Haddington branch. D34 No. 2471 *Glen Falloch* is in the background. (J. Robertson Collection/Colour Rail)

Only twelve of this saturated 'intermediate' design were built by Reid for the NBR in 1909-10 and ten examples (all by then superheated) were still working at Nationalisation. They were the middle series of NBR K class locos classified D33 by the LNER. No. 62464 (1/10-9/53) stands outside Haymarket shed on 13th September 1953. The tender is still lettered LNER and the livery is plain black, despite nearly five years of BR ownership. No. 62464 was based at Dunfermline (62C) and only a matter of days away from withdrawal. It was the last member of the class. Behind is D11/2 *Lord Glenallan* (10/24-9/58) note the Scottish style curved handrail on both smokebox doors. (J. Robertson/Colour Rail)

Right: The first Glen No. 62467 *Glenfinnan,* built at Cowlairs in September 1913 and withdrawn in August 1960, approaches Dalmeny Junction with a southbound evening Edinburgh local in the early-mid 1950s. Dalmeny station and the Forth Bridge are visible in the background. No. 62467 was a Thornton Junction (62A) loco and remained so until withdrawal. The train appears to be a standard 4-coach LNER non-corridor formation, strengthened at the front by an LNER (possibly ex-GNR) corridor third and (leading), an ex-LMS non-corridor third. (Eric Treacy/Millbrook House Collection)

Left: The last series of Reid's (superheated) K class 4-4-0s, the Glens, (LNER D34) proved to be the most successful with 32 examples built between 1913 and 1920; British Railways inherited all but two of them. The arrival of the B1s and subsequent withdrawal of many earlier types of NBR 4-4-0 saw the Glens gradually being pushed on to less arduous duties, including assisting heavier southbound trains up Cockburnspath bank from Dunbar (where bankers were sub-shedded) to Grantshouse. Here No. 62471 *Glen Falloch* (10/13-3/60) of St. Margarets shed (64A) pilots A2 Pacific No. 60530 *Sayajirao* (3/48-11/66) from Haymarket shed (64B) with an up express at Penmanshiel on 1st September 1956. There are holes drilled in No. 62471's buffer plank for fitting a small snowplough. (J. Robertson/Colour Rail)

Above: No. 62496 *Glen Loy* (8/20-11/61) of Eastfield (65A) and No. 62471 *Glen Falloch* (10/13-3/60) of St. Margarets (64A) take advantage of the two water cranes at Crianlarich (the West Highland was used to double heading) whilst working the 2.56 pm Fort William to Glasgow on 9th May 1959. The engines were specially rostered on the 8th and 9th of May in connection with the Railway Roundabout BBC TV series. The Eastfield Glens were almost entirely confined to freight working by this date. Both received special attention for the trips with silver paint liberally applied and red painted coupling rods.

Left: Two Glens from Fort William. A view out of the fireman's side of No. 62496 *Glen Loy's* cab as the 2.56 pm climbs towards Spean Bridge. (P. B. Whitehouse/Millbrook House Collection) - both)

Gresley's 'Shires' and 'Hunts'

The idea behind the D49s was to produce a modern design to cover secondary duties and cross country trains in Scotland and the North East, together with routes where the Pacifics were barred. There were several such restrictions at the time of design (e.g. the Waverley Route) which were later upgraded; this robbed the class of their *raison d'etre* particularly in Scotland. The first batch of this three-cylinder design had Walschaerts valve gear, with Gresley derived motion for the middle cylinder. They went to Scotland and by Nationalisation worked duties such as Edinburgh-Glasgow trains.

The 'Shire' naming theme was the earlier to be adopted with the Walschaerts engines, the 'Hunt' names appearing later with the Lentz poppet valve series, and there is a fair amount of evidence that Gresley left much of the detail design work to Darlington. The engines certainly had a sort of 'North Eastern' flavour to them and this was re-inforced by their principal areas of operation, particularly the 'Hunts'.

These later Lentz rotary cam poppet valve geared locomotives (some earlier 'Shires' received an oscillating cam version but were later rebuilt as Walschaerts engines) were largely based in the North East, an area which had an abundance of medium distance express duties such as Leeds-Hull, Newcastle-Carlisle and Scarborough-York-Leeds. They continued on these trains until the influx of the BR Modernisation Plan DMUs ousted them, no doubt to the relief of enginemen and passengers alike, as their harsh riding qualities were notorious. With 6ft 8in driving wheels and a 21 ton axle load, their sphere of operation was limited; consequently they disappeared very quickly, many of them vanishing from the scene several years prior to their older pre-Grouping sisters.

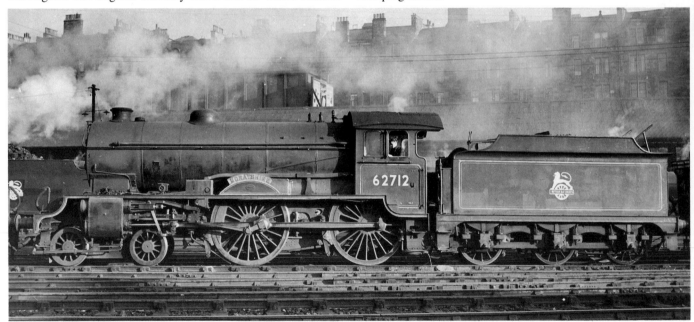

Above: A fine portrait of D49/1 No. 62712 *Morayshire* (2/28-7/61) now preserved, taken at St. Margarets shed (64A), Edinburgh on 23rd May 1952 shows the long wheel base and somewhat ungainly proportions of this Gresley product. The locomotive is in BR lined black livery with the route availability number low down on the cab side (in this case RA 8). Behind No. 62712's smokebox, the tender to an unknown loco has just had British Railways in full painted over and the early BR crest substituted. The 'Shire's' GCR pattern tender also shows signs of patch painting and repair. Note that the 2:1 rocking lever for the derived motion of the inside cylinder valves is behind the cylinders, not in front as on the Gresley Pacifics. (J. Robertson Collection/Colour Rail)

Left: Double headed D49/2s (No. 62726 *The Meynell* (3/29-12/57), the first of the Lentz rotary cam poppet valve type originally named *Leicestershire* in the lead), take a southbound express out of York in the mid 1950s. 50E is Scarborough shed, where No. 62726 remained until withdrawal. The locomotives are coupled to two different types of LNER standard tender with stepped out and straight sides. The stock is mostly LMS with an LMR porthole Brake Third leading. (Eric Treacy/Millbrook House Collection)

Below: No. 62736 *The Bramham Moor* (4/32-6/58) of Starbeck shed (50D) in filthy condition heads south, in the cutting through the Stray at Harrogate, with the 2.20 pm Harrogate-Kings Cross express on 29th April 1956. The leading coaches, in BR red and cream, are all Thompson corridor designs, a 4 compartment brake third, two thirds and a first. The Leeds-Harrogate-Ripon-North-allerton line (now sadly closed beyond Harrogate) was one of the most familiar venues for these engines, several of which were shedded at Starbeck, some 2-3 miles out of Harrogate in the York direction. (T. J. Edgington)

Above: The crew of Starbeck (50D), Harrogate based D49/2 No. 62773 *The South Durham* (1/35-8/58) await the right away from Leeds City piloting a B1 4-6-0 with a Liverpool-Newcastle express (via Harrogate and Ripon) in 1950. No. 62773 is immaculately turned out in BR lined black with red backed nameplate. The pilot would be required for the difficult 18 miles to Harrogate via Arthington, including some 4½ miles at around 1:100, ending between Horsforth and Bramhope Tunnel. (Eric Treacy/Millbrook House Collection)

Right: No. 62764 *The Garth* (10/34-11/58) stands on the Rugby Test Plant in May 1949 whilst undergoing trials of its Reidinger valve gear. Tests with this type of valve gear had started in 1939 on No. 365 *The Morpeth* but it was removed and stored in 1941; *The Morpeth* was then rebuilt by Thompson into the inside cylindered class D. The Reidinger valve gear gave an infinitely variable cut-off to the rotary cam poppet valve gear whereas the Lentz gear fitted to the 'Hunts' had only 5 (later series had 7) cut-off positions in forward gear, making the ideal setting for economic running more difficult than with a conventional Walschaerts gear. In February 1949 No. 62764 was fitted with a modified version of the infinitely variable gear taken from No. 365, which it retained until withdrawal. No other members of the class were altered. (J. M. Jarvis)

Left: Class D. The Solitary Thompson rebuild of D49/2 No. 2768 *The Morpeth* (12/34 rebuilt 8/42-11/52) of Starbeck shed waits at York platform 13 with a local for Harrogate via Poppleton on 21st May 1948; the leading carriage is of NER origin. The locomotive, rebuilt with inside cylinders similar to the GC D11 pattern, was not a conspicuous success and worked mainly local services around Leeds and Harrogate via Arthington, Wetherby and York. As BR No. 62768, it was withdrawn after a shunting accident. There is evidence of wartime damage in the lack of glass in the canopies and overall roof. Semaphore signals are still in place and on the platform behind the locomotive a water cart for provisioning dining cars with drinking water can be seen. (P. M. Alexander/Millbrook House Collection)

The Great Western 'Bulldogs'

The Great Western's motive power revolution came with G. J. Churchward but various classes of 4-4-0 continued to be built during the early years of the great man's reign, all of them double framed, something regarded as old fashioned even then. Introduced in 1898 the 5ft 8in wheel 'Bulldog' Class was turned out from Swindon until 1910; it was a useful intermediate engine capable of express, stopping train or freight work and it spread over most of the system except for the 'yellow' or 'uncoloured' routes.

In later GWR days its nose was put out of joint by the arrival of the new 'Manors', 'Granges' and 'Halls' and had it not been for World War II it is unlikely that any of the class would have survived the early 1940s. Few, therefore, came into the Western Region of British Railways but Worcester, Hereford, Newton Abbot and Reading had their share, the South Devon engines being used as station pilots, for local services and, mainly, as pilots over the steep inclines from Dainton to Plymouth. By 1951 they were all gone.

Above: London 'Bulldog'. No. 3364 *Frank Bibby* (2/03-6/49 and named *Bibby* to 4/03) stands at Old Oak Common shed on 5th December 1948. This was a Westbury (WES) engine during the whole of its BR period. A number of 'Bulldogs' were kept in the London Division to work the Didcot-Winchester route until the Class 53XX Moguls became available; what No. 3364 was doing in London at the time is not known. (P. M. Alexander/Millbrook House Collection)

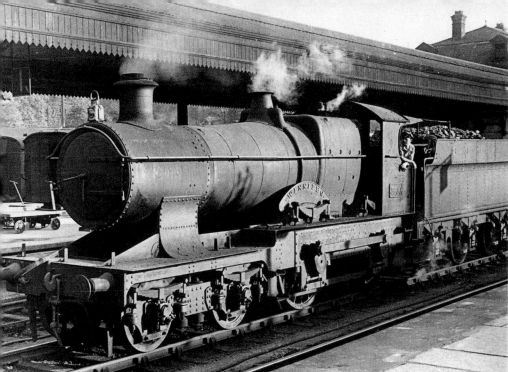

Left: Station pilot: sixteen 'Bulldogs' were part of the Newton Abbot Division at Nationalisation; this included five allocated to Newton Abbot shed, mainly for piloting and banking duties on the South Devon inclines. No. 3400 *Winnipeg* (2/04-5/49) does a turn at Exeter St. Davids on 25th August 1948. It was withdrawn from Exeter shed (EXE). (P. M. Alexander/Millbrook House Collection)

Below: Far from home: one of the later 'Bulldogs', No. 3451 *Pelican* (1/10-4/51), then allocated to Exeter (EXE), runs south through Hereford at the head of a north to west freight on 6th November 1948, a sad comedown for a once smart engine. As with most of the class right up to withdrawal there is no sign of BR ownership. (P. M. Alexander/Millbrook House Collection)

Working home: No. 3341 *Blasius* (5/00-11/49), fitted with a cast iron chimney and one of three members of its class to carry a smokebox door plate (Nos. 3432 and 3453 were the others), leaves Exeter St. Davids with a stopping train for Newton Abbot on 31st August 1949. It was then a Newton Abbot (NA) engine. The building on the left is one of the old pumping stations for the South Devon Railway's atmospheric system used by Brunel in 1847-8. (P. M. Alexander/Millbrook House Collection)

'Bulldog' at rest: No. 3401 *Vancouver* (3/04-11/49) at Hereford shed (HFD) on 6th November 1948. The Hereford and Worcester 'Bulldogs' were used on a variety of services: stopping trains on the west to north route, locals to Worcester, Stratford and either Leamington or Birmingham and also on freights. Once the new 'Halls' came into service, their days were numbered. Note the Great Western turntable in the foreground. (P. M. Alexander/ Millbrook House Collection)

Above: On the main line, No. 3419 (6/06-8/49 and unnamed) finds a thirty nine wagon train hard work as it passes over Goring troughs, on 15th August 1949, only days before withdrawal. It was a Didcot engine to which it had been recently transferred from Winchester (a sub shed of Didcot, therefore coded DID), after being displaced by the 53XX 2-6-0s. (P. M. Alexander/Millbrook House Collection)

Right: *Skylark* No. 3454 (1/10-11/51) was a 'Bulldog' and is seen here at Snow Hill station Birmingham on the down through road prior to picking up its passengers for a Stephenson Locomotive Society special to Swindon works. It is 17th June 1951 and the whole train is Great Western. Nos. 3453 *Seagull* and 3454 *Skylark* were the last members of the class to remain in service; they were withdrawn from Reading shed (81D) on the same day. (P. B. Whitehouse/Millbrook House Collection)

Left: The end of the line. An appearance in Swindon works stock shed officially meant that an engine was in store, but for many it was but a step to the scrap road. The engine to the left of the picture, taken on 29th September 1948, is No. 3377 (5/03-3/51) and to the right is No. 3444 *Cormorant* (5/09-6/51), officially a Taunton loco. Both these engines were lucky and would see the light of day again by Spring 1950. (P. M. Alexander/ Millbrook House Collection)

Above: All stations to Worcester. No. 3377 (5/03-3/51) originally named *Penzance*) breasts the summit of Hatton bank with the 11.27 am ex Leamington Spa stopping at all stations. The route is via Hatton Junction, Bearley Junction, Stratford upon Avon, Honeybourne and Evesham. It is 15th April 1950 and No. 3377 has only recently been transferred to Worcester shed (whence it was withdrawn) from Shrewsbury. This is one of a number of 'Bulldogs' stripped of their names around 1927/30 'to avoid confusion with train destinations'. Either passengers in those times were particularly stupid or the Great Western equally so! No. 3377 had this unwelcome treatment in August 1930 having confused the public for over 27 years! It was one of nine 'Bulldogs' stationed at Worcester (WOS) at the time. The locomotive is lettered 'British Railways' in GWR style characters on the tender. (P. M. Alexander/Millbrook House Collection)

The first 'Bulldogs' were built prior to the introduction of the Churchward curved nameplate carried over the engine's leading (4-4-0) or centre (4-6-0) splasher. Nos. 3320-60 all had oval combined name and number plates on the cab sides. Nos. 3320-5/40 were more elaborate having the GWR coat of arms as a central feature. No. 3320 was supplied with the new 'standard' type plates in 1903.

In the first view, the nameplate of No. 3340 *Camel* (10/99-6/34) shows the inset GWR coat of arms while the next picture, No. 3337 *The Wolf* (3/00-5/34), shows the standard cabside combined number and nameplate. On both plates it is worth noting that the works number is still extant but the date of building had been obliterated. The final detail view shows the more familiar standard curved plate over the splasher of No. 3401 *Vancouver* (3/04-11/49). (P. M. Alexander/Millbrook House Collection)

The South Eastern & Chatham legacy

One reason for the longevity of many 4-4-0 designs on the old Southern Railway was the fact that the Southern's electrification programme absorbed much of the company's time and resources leaving relatively little opportunity for steam locomotive development on the LMS/LNER/GWR scale. Maunsell was, nonetheless, a fine engineer and introduced some splendid designs, but he also had to keep (proportionally) more of the 'old-timers' going than was the case elsewhere. He was an ex-SE&CR man, so it seems quite appropriate that in this first volume of our four-coupled survey, we should first take a look at the many varied (and often quite excellent) products of his old company.

On its absorption into the Southern Railway the South Eastern and Chatham did not possess a single six coupled express tender engine. It did, however, have a number of rebuilt and superheated 4-4-0s and a comparatively new (1914) 4-4-0 in class L. With Maunsell taking over the CME's job and the proved efficiency of the engines, he built a further series known as the L1 in 1926. Right up until their demise, occasioned by electrification at the end of the 1950s, the D1, E1, L and L1 4-4-0s were used on the Kent Coast trains (many of them expresses), and it can truthfully be said that they were amongst the most successful inside cylinder four coupled engines ever built.

Some of the original D and E class were not rebuilt and these engines, dating from 1906 worked their time out until the mid 1950s. A few (very few) of the earlier South Eastern Railway rebuilt Stirling 4-4-0s of Classes F1 and B1 also came into BR ownership spending their last days on the Reading-Guildford-Redhill services. Both were gone by 1951.

Left: Reading based Stirling class F1 No. 1105 (3/96-1/49) approaches St. Catherines Tunnel south of Guildford on 3rd September 1948. This is a Redhill-Guildford-Reading train which has just joined the Portsmouth direct line at Shalford Junction. Even in their latter days, these F1 Class 4-4-0s still retained some visual linkages with the same designer's earlier 4-4-0s for the Glasgow and South Western Railway – mostly scrapped by the LMS a generation earlier. (P. M. Alexander/Millbrook House Collection)

Above: SER class F1 4-4-0 No. 31151 (10/89-2/49) leaves Guildford on the 1.25 pm to Reading on 3rd February 1949 only days before withdrawal. The stock is a Maunsell three coach corridor set with a four wheel luggage van bringing up the rear. The Southern Region was quick off the mark with locomotive renumbering after 1947, albeit usually associated with hybrid liveries. No. 31151 was the only F1 to receive the 3 prefix and was withdrawn from Reading shed. (P. M. Alexander/Millbrook House Collection)

Below: South Eastern Railway class B1 No. 1448 (8/98-9/49) of Reading (south) shed, later (70E), near Shalford the last station before Guildford on the SER line from Redhill. The train is the 12.00 noon from Redhill to Reading on 15th March 1949. It seems to be the usual three coach corridor set plus a van. The engine is seen carrying the post war Southern plain black livery with Bulleid's 'Sunshine' insignia. (P. M. Alexander/Millbrook House Collection)

Above: Harry Wainwright's Class D 4-4-0s were a celebrated type and in this view, one of the Ashford built 1907 batch of Ds, No. 31477 (3/07-1/51) stands in Wye station (between Canterbury West and Ashford) with a Margate-Charing Cross train in June 1950. The D (still with 'Southern' and the number of a previous engine No. 1738 on the tender) would work to Ashford (its home shed) where the coaches were attached to a Ramsgate-Charing Cross train via Dover. The train is made up of a Bulleid 4-coach corridor set introduced after the war with semi-open brake thirds at each end and with two vans of patently SE&CR inspiration bringing up the rear. (D. Cross)

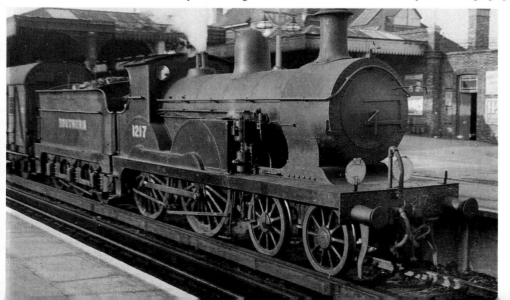

Left: No. 1217 (10/98-6/50) of Reading shed, the penultimate Stirling B1 to be withdrawn, stands at Guildford station with what appears to be a train for the Horsham line c1949. (The 5.05 pm Reading-Guildford train formed the 6.34 pm Guildford-Cranleigh). This is a truly late-Victorian machine, the deep footplate valancing, short wheel base bogie and somewhat archaic tender (with external handrail) all being redolent of the earlier Stirling era on the GSWR. It would have looked quite 'at home' at Glasgow St. Enoch some 50 or more years earlier! (P. M. Alexander/Millbrook House Collection)

Above: The 6.34 pm Guildford-Cranleigh passes Peasmarsh Junction and runs onto the line to Christ's Hospital on 21st July 1950. The engine is class D No. 31744 (5/03-4/53). The train originated at Reading at 5.05 pm and the stock is an ex SE&CR three-coach 'birdcage' set. This unusual picture shows an SE&CR locomotive leaving the LSWR Portsmouth main line for the LB&SCR Horsham branch. No. 31744 was one of five Ds based at Reading (South) at this date, following the withdrawal of the older Stirling F1s and B1s. (P. M. Alexander/Mill-brook House Collection)

Right: Reading Southern shed (70E) in 1953 with class D No. 31075 (3/03-12/56) in the centre about to work an afternoon train to Guildford and Redhill. To the left and right are 2-6-0s of class N Nos. 31827 (5/24-9/63) and 31865 (6/25-9/63) which had taken some of the Redhill turns from 4-4-0s. The shed became little more than a servicing point in May 1954 when the majority of its allocation was transferred away; however it was not demoted to sub-shed status until 1959 with final closure coming in 1965. (P. B. Whitehouse/Millbrook House Collection)

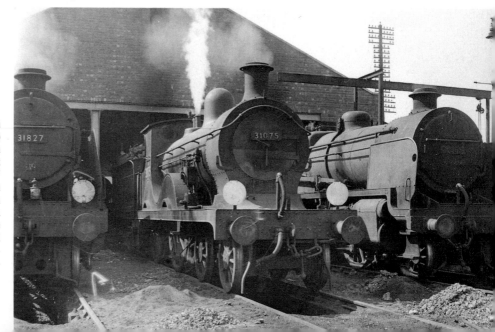

Left: During the 1950s BR was not always too cost-conscious and many exotic locomotives were often brought from distant sheds to work enthusiast's special trains. One such was SECR D class 4-4-0 No. 31075 (3/03-12/56) which, double headed with GWR Dean Goods No. 2538, worked the Talyllyn Railway Preservation Society's AGM special from Shrewsbury to Towyn on 22nd September 1956. This unlikely couple are seen here at Welshpool during a water stop. (P. B. Whitehouse/Millbrook House Collection)

Right: The Wainwright Ds were undeniably handsome engines – as any who have seen the preserved No. 737 at the National Railway Museum will agree. They combined form and function in a most agreeable way and even in BR days, devoid of their earlier Edwardian decorative finery, their classic lines always won through. This is very clearly seen in this fine portrait study of SECR Class D 4-4-0 No. 31549 (9/06-10/56) at Ashford shed (74A), its home depot, in the early 1950s. This was one of 11 engines built at Ashford works in 1906/7 which had rectangular cab cab windows in addition to the normal circular ones. (P. B. Whitehouse/ Millbrook House Collection)

Above: The Class E 4-4-0s followed the Ds and, if not quite so handsome of form, were probably rather better engines. In this view, Class E No. 1273 (2/06-10/51) leaves Guildford at the head of the 1.15 pm to Redhill on 8th April 1948. Still in Southern wartime black with 'sunshine' letters. No. 1273 was one of four members of its class to receive the BR lined black livery, in September 1949 when renumbered 31273. The leading vehicle is one of the rather austere but by no means disagreeable late period SE&CR non-corridors. (P. M. Alexander/Millbrook House Collection)

Left: One of the twelve Class L 4-4-0s built by Beyer Peacock & Co. at Gorton, Manchester, No. 31767 (9/14-10/58) of St. Leonards shed (74E) in SR Malachite green but with 'British Railways' in full 'sunshine' lettering on the tender, a livery it kept until February 1954, at Mountfield on the 11.28 am Tonbridge-Hastings on 16th September 1952. The coaches are special 'Restriction 1' narrow stock for the Hastings line. This stock was confined to 8ft width because of tight clearances in tunnels. On the left is a train from the local gypsum mines hauled by one of the firm's locos, possibly *Kemp*, an 0-6-ST built by Andrew Barclay & Co. of Kilmarnock. (P. M. Alexander/Millbrook House Collection)

Above: Beyer Peacock built class L 4-4-0 No. 31770 (9/14-11/59) hauling the 2.06 pm Rye-Hastings-Tonbridge local near Wadhurst on 20th September 1952. The locomotive is in BR lined black whose tidy application was rather marred as a result of the presence of a horizontal handrail along the cabside. The stock is an ex-SE&CR 'Birdcage' set in BR lined crimson livery; the lining is applied rather too low down to be effective. Though now based at Tonbridge, the engine still carries the Eastleigh (71A) shed code having worked from there between December 1951 and August 1952. (P. M. Alexander/Millbrook House Collection)

Above: Ten Class Ls were built by A. Borsig & Co. of Berlin for the South Eastern & Chatham Railway just prior to World War I. They were probably the only German-built locomotives to be ordered for any British railway company. No. 31776 (6/14-2/61) of Brighton shed (75A) leaves Tunbridge Wells West with a Brighton train in February 1960, a service it had worked since transfer to Brighton in 1956. The locomotive is still in lined black livery but carries the second BR crest. On the right is BR Class 4 4-6-0 No. 75074 on a London (Victoria) train whilst on shed to the left are K Class 2-6-0 No. 32347 and an unidentified Class Q1 0-6-0. (D. Cross)

Right: Because of their origins the SE&CR L class engines were nicknamed 'Germans'. No. 31777 (6/14-9/59) sits on the vacuum operated turntable at Ashford c1953. This has a logical arrangement of the lining which follows the splashers but thereby moving the numbers higher up the cabside, which is lined only in red. Note the steam reversing gear ahead of the right hand leading splasher. This was originally designed by James Stirling on the SER and fitted to all the Southern Region 4-4-0s covered in this volume. (P. B. Whitehouse/Millbrook House Collection)

Below: A Hastings train emerges from Elmstead Woods Tunnel headed by class D1 No. 31735 (1/02-rebuilt 8/21-4/61) around May 1959. The set seen here, No. 190, was a four-coach formation (Brake Third, two composites, Brake Third) built in 1931 as part of the last 8ft 6in wide carriage sets built by the Southern Railway and originally intended for use on the Eastern Section to such destinations as Folkestone, Deal, Eastbourne and Hastings. Restricted width stock was always a feature of the SR before and after the war and undoubtedly prevented larger-scale standardisation during Maunsell's time. The D1s originally had plain coupling rods but the E1s and L1s had fluted rods – one of the recognition factors for these very similar engines. No. 31735 was shedded at Bricklayers Arms (73B); following the Kent Coast electrification in June 1959 it was transferred to the Western Section where it remained until withdrawal. Eastleigh works scrapped the locomotive. (D. Cross)

Left: Rebuilt class D1 No. 31487 (7/02 rebuilt 5/21-2/61) leaving Tonbridge and climbing on gradients mostly between 1:90 and 1:100, after an initial 1:53 round the curve out of the station, to Tunbridge Wells with a Hastings train composed of three 'narrow' corridor coaches. These 8ft wide carriages were built in 1930-31 for London, Bexhill and Hastings services. Four three-coach sets (Third Brake, First, Third Brake) were built at the time of which No. 213, illustrated, was the first to emerge. The date of the picture is around 1959 or 1960 although the 74D shed plate for Tonbridge should have changed to 73J from 1958. The signal post, partially obscured by steam, is constructed of old rails – a typical Southern economy. (D. Cross)

Below: D1 No. 31739 (1/02-rebuilt 4/27-11/61) of Bricklayers Arms (73B) climbs to Goudhurst (on the Hawkhurst branch from Paddock Wood) with the empty stock for a return special. This appears to be a mixture of push-pull sets plus some corridors. The vans marshalled between the coaches suggest that it is a return hop-pickers special. On withdrawal, No. 31739 had achieved the highest mileage of any Wainwright 4-4-0: 2,002,974. The photograph was taken near Church Lane Siding on 20th September 1953. (S. C. Nash)

Above: Towards the end of their lives, the D1s were used on various parcels trains, ramblers specials and the like. No. 31749 (10/03 – rebuilt at Beyer Peacock 11/21-11/61) is seen here on such a turn, the Benenden School special on 2nd May 1961, the start of the summer term. The train ran from Charing Cross to Cranbrook and this is the empty stock returning to London. Note the SECR signal above the fifth coach. No. 31749 spent its last 2½ years at Bricklayers Arms (73B). (S. C. Nash)

Right: Stewarts Lane (73A) based Class E1 No. 31504 (2/06-rebuilt 4/20-2/58) emerges from Penge Tunnel and approaches Sydenham Hill station on 19th August 1950 with an up Ramsgate train. The figures on the top disc represent the locomotive duty number for the shed whilst the numbers on the oblong board represent the reporting number for the train. The leading vehicle is one of the 8ft 6in wide 'Continental' carriages built for the SR to a basically SE&CR design shortly after the 1923 grouping. (P. M. Alexander/Millbrook House Collection)

Class E1 No. 31019 (7/08-rebuilt 2/20-4/61) enters Tonbridge on 15th August 1955 with an RCTS special train, 'The Wealden Limited', which traversed inter-alia the 'Bluebell' line after closure on 28th May 1955 and before its reopening in 1956. The stock is a mixture of Hastings line brakes and Pullman buffet (fourth from engine) plus the 1921 design continental coaches (second and third vehicles). Tonbridge is a centre for the manufacture of cricket equipment and one such, T. Ives & Son Ltd., Cricket Ball Manufacturers, is visible above the locomotive. No. 31019 was allocated to the former SE&C depot at Stewarts Lane (73A). (P. B. Whitehouse/Millbrook House Collection)

A regular job for the superheated 4-4-0s was as pilot either to another 4-4-0 or to a 4-6-2 on the 'Night Ferry'. Class L1 No. 31754 (3/26-11/61) double heads 'Battle of Britain' Class 4-6-2 No. 34070 *Manston* (11/47-8/64) at Bickley Junction on the up train c1958. Both locomotives were based at Dover shed (74C, 73H from September 1958). The train was one of the heaviest in the country with Wagon-Lits sleeping cars from Paris and Brussels plus fourgons (continental luggage vans). At least 12 coaches plus 2 fourgons can be seen in this picture of what was the only regular sleeping car working on SR routes. At the time of the picture, extensive engineering work was in progress in preparation for the Kent Coast electrification. (D. Cross)

Although an Eastern Section design the L1s appeared elsewhere and here No. 31786 (4/26-2/62) approaches Lyndhurst Road with a Lymington-Southampton local on 4th April 1953. The locomotive had only been repainted from malachite green in January, having been transferred to Eastleigh in December 1952; it has not received a new shed plate. The carriages are characteristic LSWR non-corridors. (P. M. Alexander/Millbrook House Collection)

The L1 4-4-0s (like the D1s and E1s) all bore a strong family likeness and also displayed more than a passing resemblance to the Midland/LMS Class 2P 4-4-0s. This was largely because of the influence of James Clayton, Maunsell's Chief Draughtsman on the SR, who had learned much of his 'trade' at Derby (ex-MR).

This outward style is well exemplified in this view of Class L1 No. 31758 (3/26-10/59), Ashford (74A) based, running light engine from Margate to Ramsgate at Dumpton Park in May 1957. The locomotive has probably worked a London-Margate train and is running to Ramsgate shed for servicing. Even the tender has a 'Midland' look to it and the view forms an appropriate link to the second volume in our four-coupled survey, wherein the Midland/LMS Class 2Ps will be featured. (P. B. Whitehouse/Millbrook House Collection)

Bibliography

Locomotives of the Great Western Railway, RCTS, 1951 onwards.
Locomotives of the London & North Eastern Railway, RCTS, 1963 onwards.
The Locomotive History of the South Eastern Railway, D. C. Bradley. RCTS, 1985 edition.

The Locomotive History of the South Eastern & Chatham Railway, D. L. Bradley, RCTS, 1980 edition.
The Locomotive Stock Book, RCTS, various years.
The Stephenson Locomotive Society Journal, volumes covering 1948-63.
The Midland Compounds, D. F. Tee, RCTS, 1962.